MAUSOLEA
HIBERNICA

Maurice Craig
&
Michael Craig

THE LILLIPUT PRESS

Fine Arts

NB
1805
C73
1999

First published 1999 by The Lilliput Press Ltd, 62–63 Sitric Road, Arbour Hill, Dublin 7, Ireland.

A CIP record for this title is available from the British Library.

ISBN 1 901866 30 0

The Lilliput Press receives financial assistance from An Chomhairle Ealaíon / The Arts Council of Ireland.

The authors gratefully acknowledge the School of Irish Studies Foundation for its financial support of this publication.

Set in 12 on 14 Monotype Centaur

Printed in Ireland by Betaprint of Dublin

Fine Arts

MAUSOLEA
HIBERNICA

CONTENTS

VIGNETTES

PREFACE AND ACKNOWLEDGMENTS

This book is not a guide book; still less is it an academic or comprehensive treatment of the subject. It is a picture book. Its purpose is to give the reader some of the pleasure which the authors have had in seeking these buildings, in finding and recording them. It is intended as an anthology and to represent, as far as possible, their spread in space and time, and the variety of their styles. Some are well cared for; others are utterly neglected, ruinous and overgrown; many are in that optimum but transient condition known as 'pleasing decay', and these have pleased us most.

Thanks for help in various ways are due to: the late Walter Armytage, Christine Casey, Marcus Clements, Sir Howard Colvin, Con Costello, James S. Curl, Ruth Delany, Luke Dodd, the late N.W. English, William Garner, the Knight of Glin, David Griffin, D. Hardy, James Howley, David N. Johnson, J.

Joyce, R. Loeber, the late A.K. Longfield, A. McCoy, J. McCullough, E. McParland, P. Melvin, the late Vivian Mercier, J. O'Connell, R. O'Donnell, the Countess of Rosse, Alistair Rowan, Etienne Rynne, Jeanne Sheehy, C. Saumarez Smith, Jeremy Williams, S. Walford, the late H.A. Wheeler; and Bernard and Mary Loughlin and the staff of the Tyrone Guthrie Centre at Annaghmakerrig for hospitality and encouragement.

The two principal works in English on the subject are: *A Celebration of Death* by James Stevens Curl (1980) and *Architecture and the After-Life* by Howard Colvin (1991). In James Howley's *The Follies and Garden Buildings of Ireland* (1993), Chapter 10 is devoted to mausoleums, while two minor prolegomena are 'Mausoleums in Ireland', a preliminary handlist by Maurice Craig, in *Studies,* Winter 1975, and *Mausolea in Ulster* by J.S. Curl (1978). Homan Potterton's *Irish Church Monuments* (1975) deals with a cognate but distinct topic.

INTRODUCTION

VALDE ENIM FALSUM EST VIVO
QUIDEM DOMOS CULTAS ESSE,
NON CURARI EAS, UBI DIUTIUS
NOBIS HABITANDUM EST

Petr. Satyr. LXXI

Ireland, it has often been remarked, is a land of graveyards. Graveyards, be it noted, rather than churchyards or cemeteries. All the graveyards I have in mind once contained a church, sometimes more than one church, represented today, if at all, only by a ragged piece of wall or maybe a gable. Cemeteries, by contrast, are rectilinear, with or without a chapel at the gates, usually in or near towns, and are always a creation of the last century and a half.

'Personally,' says Samuel Beckett, 'I have no bone to pick with graveyards, I take the air there willingly, perhaps more willingly than elsewhere, when take the air I must. My sandwich, my banana, taste sweeter when I'm sitting on a tomb …' And Sir Thomas Browne goes further: 'I could digest a Sallad gathered in a Churchyard, as well as in a Garden.' But it is Joyce who, in a very few words, best adumbrates the essence of the Irish graveyard, with 'the moongrey nettles, the black mould and the muttering rain'.

In some of these graveyards the only roofed building may be somebody's mausoleum. So perhaps it is time for a definition. Some years ago I attempted one which the most distinguished of my contemporaries has done me the honour to adopt: 'A funerary structure having the character of a roofed building, and large enough to stand up in, or at least having that appearance.' In a great many instances the doorway, though more or less of human scale, is wholly or partly below ground level. In the very grand mausoleum at Kiltegan there are steps down to the entrance, whereas at Ruan and Killadysert—which, though grand, are no grander—everything appears to be above ground. In this, as in other respects as well, the spirit of compromise (surprisingly since this is Ireland) may be seen at work.

Until very lately it was a not uncommon experience to find the door ajar and to walk in and find all the coffins on the floor or stacked on shelves. But within the last few years, no doubt as a result of increased mobility and hence of vandalism, and the decay of traditional pieties, doorways have been bricked or cemented up. The elaborate mausoleum at Rossmore, Co. Monaghan, for example, was recently vandalized, so that the coffins have had to be reburied elsewhere.

To digress for a moment, there is in Mount Jerome a tomb (not quite a mausoleum) which was surmounted, until its recent mutilation by vandals, by a rather larger than life-size statue of a dog, while in a small aperture at eye-height one could look through to a small stained-glass eyelet in the opposite wall depicting, in colour, the same dog standing on its master's coffin, howling to the heavens. But that, too, is no longer to be seen, though I had the sense to make a colour slide of it while it could still be done. Trimalchio, it will be recalled, implored Habinnas the monumental mason 'to have the pup carved at the feet of my statue' when he was specifying the dimensions and amenities of his final home.

Mausolea vary greatly in size and pretension, from the almost shapeless lumps of stonework with a door half under ground, to such a full-blown memorial church as that of Myshall in Co. Carlow, which, except for the explicit dedication to the young girl whose statue it contains, is in all respects like any other church of its period, though unusually large and elaborate, and it is in fact the parish church. The mausolea or memorial chapels of Bianconi at Boherlahan or of the Grace family at Arless lie somewhere towards that end of the spectrum.

There are some early Irish buildings that may claim to be mausolea. It seems very likely that those small stone-built Early Christian 'oratories', which go by such names as 'St Molaga's Bed' (Labbamolaga) or St Molaise's 'House' on Devenish Island, were their final resting places rather than their habitations during life. Though they are large enough to function as chapels, and people no doubt prayed in them, they are obviously first cousins to those solid examples, of sub-human scale, which are found in similar contexts, for example, at Corran, Slane, Banagher, Bovevagh or Clones.

Though mausolea in this sense seem to have died out during the Middle Ages, and they have little or no part to play in the origins of the modern mausoleum, the Celtic Revival from the mid-nineteenth century onwards brought them into the picture. Such a building as the Hume mausoleum at Kiltegan is clearly influenced by the early examples, though nothing very like it existed in the mediæval period. But the O'Growney tomb at Maynooth by William Scott is, appropriately enough, a virtual transcription of those mentioned above, and a very faithful one ...

Much of the devotional life of mediæval Ireland was centred on the friaries, which often contained elaborate tombs, as at Kilconnell, Co. Galway, Straide, Co. Mayo, or Dungiven, Co. Derry. The word 'chantry' can mean either a formal endowment to ensure the saying of masses for the dead, or the building in which such a function is performed, which building can be, and in England often is, itself inside another building, and even have a roof of its own. Nothing quite like that seems to be known in Ireland, if only because none of the cathedrals was large enough to accommodate them.

THE REFORMATION did not take effect all at once, particularly not in the west of Ireland, where some friaries lingered on or were re-occupied in the seventeenth and even the early eighteenth centuries, under the protection of such families as the Clanrickarde Burkes or the Nugents of Pallas. Prominent Catholic families appropriated parts of friary and abbey churches, such as transepts and side-chapels, as their exclusive burial places, and sometimes furnished them with an altar. Sometimes they merely inserted a large vault of their own into part of the church, and in some cases provided it with a more or less architectural frontispiece. There are examples at Kilmallock, Killone, Bonamargy, Corcomroe and elsewhere.

Whether this was done while the friary or abbey was still (or again) a going concern and roofed, or after it had become a ruin, is not always easy to determine. Almost certainly both were done. At Kinelekin (commonly called 'Abbey') in Co. Galway there are two side-chapels dedicated to the Burke family, with seventeenth-century altars and monuments, and one of these has a relatively modern roof. At Kilcorban, not far away, a (perhaps pre-existing) chapel has been appropriated by the Nugents; similarly at Ballintober, Co. Mayo, also by the Burkes. In these cases it is fairly clear that the burials were under the floor and the visitor was expected to say a prayer for the departed.

From the late seventeenth century there survive a small number of mortuary chapels, apparently newly built. At Castletown-geoghegan 'This Chappel was built for James Wyer in memor of his son David Wyer 1671'; at Kilkenny West not far from Athlone a barrel-vaulted structure is dated 1680 (near the grave of Goldsmith's father); at Inchyolaghan near Kilkenny a wall-monument of the Cuffe family is dated 1679 in a building which, though perhaps of earlier origin, seems to have been enlarged; similarly at Strokestown an earlier building seems to have been adapted to receive and display a monument of 1686 in a naïvely classical style.

A little apart from these, and somewhat earlier, is the remarkable building of 1637 at Rath Reagh, otherwise Fox Hall, in Co. Longford, in which the grandiose monument of Sir Nathaniel Fox, a Protestant with numerous Catholic relatives, complete with reclining effigy in full armour, occupied the centre of the north wall, while the west boasted externally a frontispiece of, for its period, remarkably pure and advanced classicism. Unquestionably the primary purpose of this building was to receive the tomb and provide a setting for the monument. But a little over a century later it was being used as a Protestant parish church and had become too small, so it was extended westwards and the frontispiece reassembled in a garbled form.

Rath Reagh was, from the beginning, in form a church. But there soon appeared a class of mausolea with a more concentrated focus, in which, typically, the visitor, facing through the door, is confronted by a monument of greater or less pretension. The pretension of the monument inside usually, but not invariably, exceeds that of its integument. While Nikolaus Pevsner undoubtedly exaggerated the external modesty of the mau-

soleum of Galla Placidia at Ravenna by liken-
ing it to a potting-shed, the better to contrast
this with its internal splendour, there are
some Irish mausolea which, in a much hum-
bler way, can show a similar contrast. The
very grand Conolly monument at Old Kil-
droghid (Celbridge), which is or was hidden
in a plain building without architectural
interest, is perhaps a special case, for this can
never have been intended to be its final setting. No doubt it was meant to show to
advantage in a church that never got built.

In perhaps its most satisfactory embodi-
ment, the marriage of the free-standing building and the sepulchral monument takes the
form of a small or not-so-small temple-like
building with a grilled doorway through
which may be seen the sculptured group,
ædicule or bust of the deceased, as at Pavlovsk
near St Petersburg, by Thomas de Thomon.
Whether the mausoleum by James Wyatt at
Dartrey, Co. Monaghan, originally had a

metal grille through which the fine group by Joseph Wilton could be seen, I do not know. By the time I first saw it, when it still had a roof, it had a solid door but the monument had been vandalized. The much smaller mausoleum at Inistioge, of Mary 'Psyche' Tighe, contains a notable sculpture of 1814–15 by Flaxman. It was seen by William Howitt in 1847, so that if there was an iron door, as there is now, someone opened it for him. It would seem to have been pointless to pay for a splendid piece of sculpture and then hide it away. At Fiddown, in the same county, an apparently pre-existing building, rather elegantly refurnished in 1749, houses several Ponsonby monuments, both earlier and later, and at Inchyolaghan, also in Co. Kilkenny, a very enigmatic structure, a domestic-looking frontispiece leads to an inner chamber with a Cuffe monument of 1697 on the north wall, one of a century later facing it, and what looks like the ghost of a third on the east wall between them.

The mausoleum of Cornelius O'Callaghan in the churchyard at Shanrahan, Co. Tipperary, is a sizeable but rather plain building in ashlar stone (except for the back wall in rubble), with a pointed door containing a very fine wrought-iron grille through which one sees the bust by Francis Sheahan in a pedimented ædicule with an inscription in Latin hexameters. At Mainham, Co. Kildare,

of which more later, there was originally, and is again, a grille through which the altar-frontal and ædicule, as well as the Browne monument of 1693 to the side, are clearly to be seen.

Among the most harmonious combinations of architectural form and sculptural interest is at Castlelyons in Co. Cork, where the architecture, by an unknown hand, and the sculpture, by Sheehan and Houghton, are matched in merit and simultaneously to be enjoyed. A poor relation of this is the Nason mausoleum at Ballynoe, clearly inspired by Castlelyons and with a wall-monument of much more perfunctory character, and another, also in the Castlelyons churchyard, in gothick and without any sculpture. It depends, as do so many things, on how much money there was to spend.

By the beginning of the seventeenth century the reluctance to bury inside churches, at

least inside churches *in use*, had been steadily gaining ground in northern Europe. Sir Howard Colvin has traced it with a wealth of illustration from, in particular, Italy, Sweden and Scotland. The reasons, or combinations of reasons, vary from country to country, and, most obviously, between Catholic and Protestant. Readers of M.R. James will recall, with a shiver, the case of 'Count Magnus'.

A GRAVE, a tomb, a mausoleum, a funerary chapel, a memorial church—these are stages in a gradation from the imperceptible merging of the cadaver with the earth, to its elevation into something apart and, in intention at least, permanent, especially if embalmed and lapped in lead. They are also stages in the scale by which, according to their means and their ambition, the few seek to set themselves apart from the many, whose dust, almost from the moment of death, becomes and remains anonymous. Since, in Ireland, the great majority of churches were, by the seventeenth century, in ruins (and have so remained), it was natural enough for prominent families to lay claim to favoured corners of such churches and make them into family burying-places with a vault and sometimes also a quasi-architectural frontispiece.

The great majority of free-standing mausolea are either in pre-existing graveyards, which they tend to dominate by their size and elaboration, or in demesnes, where they have something of the character of a garden-ornament or folly. Sometimes they partake of both of these characters, especially when an ancient graveyard lies within a demesne later enclosed. Granted that the main motive for having a mausoleum is to set yourself apart from the rest of humanity, some of those who did so must have been visited by the thought that there is something not altogether Christian about this. So why not compromise by putting the mausoleum, not quite *in* the graveyard, but as near to it 'as makes no matter', and so get the benefit, it is hoped, of the umbrella of faith when the final emergency is sounded, and the few can emerge to mingle with the rest? At Ballymore, for example, the old graveyard is within the demesne, and in sight of the house. The mausoleum stands a few feet outside the graveyard wall. Similarly at Carnalway, where the graveyard (with a still functioning church) abuts on the Harristown demesne and is just inside its gates, while the mausoleum, on private ground, is yet almost but not quite in the graveyard along with everyone else. I have noted half a dozen other examples of this kind.

A particularly splendid example of the art of getting the best of both worlds is that of the Countess of Granard, who died in 1972 at the age of ninety. The Forbes family of Castle Forbes, Co. Longford, had been, like most of their kind, Church of Ireland, but had relatively recently become Catholic. The late Countess, of whom we treat, was an American lady and was buried, not in the Catholic graveyard, nor yet, exactly, in the Protestant one. Her mausoleum is so sited, with its front wall tangential to the perimeter of the Church of Ireland graveyard at New-townforbes, that to get to it you traverse the graveyard, while the building itself is on the family's private land. It has a front elevation in what someone must have supposed to be the Greek Doric style, of blinding white marble, while the sides and back are, all too evidently, of concrete blocks.

The story behind the mausoleum at Mainham, which is on the doorstep of Clongoweswood College, is somewhat more complex. The building stands, again, just outside the graveyard in which is the old, roofless church. The mausoleum, plain though pleasing, itself of 1743, contains an altar and two tombs of about fifty years earlier, not without decorative merit, and some agreeably macabre touches. But more interesting than the tombs themselves is the story rehearsed in a 23-line inscription on a tablet over the door.

The principal tomb is that of Thomas Browne of Castle Browne (now called Clongowes), removed from St Audoen's, Dublin, by direction of Stephen Fitzwilliam Browne in 1739. He applied, we are told, several times to his parish minister, the Rev. John Daniell, for permission to put it up 'in the opposite church or adjoyning to it' but was refused 'unless said Browne would give him Five guineas for soe doing A gentleman whose character is remarkably well known as well as his behaviour on several occasions to Sd Browne & the only Clergyman in the dioces whose passion would prevent their church to be Imbelished or enlarged and to dePrive themselves & their successors From the burial fees & he has been the occasion of oblidging Sd Browne to erect Sd monument here on his own Estate of Enheritance wch Sd Browne thinks proper to incert here it was not by choice he did it may It 1743'.

By way of relief from Mr Browne's helter-skelter syntax, let us contemplate the inscription on the Clanmorris tomb at Hollymount, which is too long to have been put into the caption to plate XXX:

Beneath are mingled in their kindred dust those of her beloved parent the Rt Hon Ld Baron Clanmorris the ashes of the Hon Caroline Bingham a young lady whose exalted purity of mind personal charms and vigorous and cultivated understanding rendered her at once the delight and ornament of her family on the

20th day of April 1821 she was called to a BETTER
WORLD at the early age of 15 years, there to receive
the reward due to innocence and virtue.

Sacred to the memory of the Rt Hon Charles Smith
de Burgh Bingham Lord Baron Clanmorris of Newbrook in the County of Mayo a nobleman distinguished for the possession of those many eminent
virtues which adorn life whether we consider him in
the character of a HUSBAND FATHER LANDLORD
or FRIEND, the language of panegyric is too often
unworthily displayed in the monumental inscription
but the sincere and universal regret which still accom-
pany the recollection of this estimable NOBLEMAN
sufficiently testifies how fully he discharged his duties
both to God and Man. His lordship died on the 10th
of May 1821 in the 56th year of his age and this monument was erected by his affectionate and sorrowful
widow Baroness Clanmorris as a memorial of conjugal
affection.

In sharp contrast at Breaghwy, also in
Co. Mayo, the mausoleum consists of a circular retaining wall in the middle of a field,
with the ground inside a few feet
higher than the prevailing level,

while in the centre a rough stone structure supports an even rougher structure which at a distance looks like a much-eroded paraphrase of the Victory of Samothrace. Only the inscription—

Dom
Anne
Browne
Mort
1761

—betrays the fact that, if not a place of actual sepulture, it is a monument to the dead. It hardly qualifies by the definition quoted at the outset, but it is so remarkable that it could hardly be left out.

Standing, like it, alone in a field without apparent connexion, visual or other, with anything else, is the mausoleum at Tully, Co. Roscommon, which holds the

bones of Henry St George, junior, brother of
Sir Richard St George, Bt, who was murdered
in 1819, close by, by 'manibus nefandis'. The St
George family surely hold the palm as mau-
soleum-builders, for, besides this one, they
have the rather grand one at Carrick-on-Shannon (Hatley Manor), in a garden yet not too
far from the church, and that most poetically
sited one at Drumacoo on the wild Atlantic
shore, celebrated in verse by John Betjeman.

A SPECIAL CASE is that of the Dunraven mausoleum in the Augustinian friary at
Adare. The Dunraven (Wyndham-Quin)
family were in the early nineteenth century
still Protestant. Having restored the Trinitar-
ian church for the Catholics in 1811, they went
on to do the same for the Church of Ireland
at the Augustinian church in 1814, and there,
neatly slotted into the middle of the north
cloister arcade, is the family mausoleum.

As throughout Europe, the pyramid has always been a favoured form. Besides the three treated here as Plates there are examples at Kilcooley, Co. Tipperary, Naas (two in one graveyard), Baltinglass (of the Stratford family), Drumkeerin, Co. Leitrim (a stepped pyramid), and Kinnity, Co. Offaly (of the Bernard family). The Castlerickard pyramid is distinguished from the rest in several ways: by having three sides instead of the usual four, by being sharper and more vertical, by the altogether exceptional fineness of its masonry finish, and by its literary association.

The vast Trench mausoleum at Wood-
lawn is untypical, consisting as it does mainly
of empty space, like the enormous Delaval
mausoleum at West Wycombe. Equally
untypical is the large enclosure at Dunboden
in Co. Westmeath. Two concentric stone-
revetted circular berms, the outer some forty
feet (twelve metres) in diameter, surround a
square box containing an urn and itself
approached by a kind of tunnel, the whole
now copiously overgrown. The detail, such as
it is, is gothic.

Classical and gothic are, as might be
expected, roughly equal in favour; the gothic
sometimes tinged with romanesque and the
classical with a flavour of Egyptian, if only
with the inward-sloping jambs which, though
of fifth-century Greek origin, seem to evoke a
funerary reference. Christian iconography,
nearly always of a restrained kind, predomi-
nates, though in a few instances pagan symbols
such as the reversed torch and the shattered

column also appear. Sir Michael O'Loghlen's splendid Egyptian mausoleum has the cross on one gable and the urn on the other.

In front of the site of the now vanished great house of Summerhill, Co. Meath, a little to one side of the long straight avenue, and close to a tower-house, the mausoleum is difficult to describe and too overgrown to merit illustration. It is a large rectangle—the largest except for Woodlawn of those under review—with a shallow bow projection in one of its long sides. It may never have had a roof, and may have been, like Woodlawn, more in the nature of an enclosure than a building. Such detail as there is, in the doorway, is vaguely gothick. There are now no signs of interments. It is said by David Griffin to be by Cooley.

It is unusual for the predominant emphasis of Irish mausolea to be vertical, though Daniel O'Connell's Round Tower at Glasnevin is the conspicuous exception. It was preceded by the semi-abortive Round Tower designed by Father Horgan of Ballygibbon, Co. Cork, as a mausoleum for himself. The money ran out, so the tower began to diminish in girth about two-thirds of the way up, and never attained its full height. It bears the

dates 1836 and 1848. Later in the century there were as many Protestant 'Round Towers' as Catholic  ones, reflecting an increase in archaeological sentiment after Disestablishment in 1869. But none is of sepulchral purpose. Pearce's Stillorgan obelisk does indeed point skywards, especially since it is on the massive rockwork substructure which does not appear in his (first?) drawing, though it does have a separate drawing all to itself. The Earl-Bishop's paraphrase at Downhill, Co. Derry, of the St Rémy monument (which is not a tomb) is, or was before the top of it was blown down in

the Big Wind of 1839, as vertical as its prototype, but, like it, it is a cenotaph and not a
mausoleum. That of the Cleland family at
Dundonald, Co. Down, clearly another deriv-
ative of St Rémy, standing beside an Anglo-
Norman mote, is even more conspicuously
vertical.

A Mr Breckenridge of Clogher, Co.
Tyrone, was reputed to have been placed—
one cannot call it 'buried'—on top of a
tower, and there are similar tales, unverified,
about a Mr Beamish at De La Cour Villa near
Macroom in Co. Cork. Then there is the case
of Mr Grubb, who had himself buried standing up in the hills above Clogheen in South
Tipperary. But this is to take us beyond the
bounds of the subject.

No account, however, can possibly pass
over the strange case of Adolphus Cooke of
Cookesborough, Co. Westmeath. In the graveyard at Reynella or Rathconnell, which, like
many others, is in the middle of a field away

from the road and not very easy
of access, there is the top of a
domical vault in cut stone, surrounded by a sunken walkway
and hardly above ground level.
Beneath this vault, we are assured, reposes Mr
Cooke. But this was not his first choice. During his lifetime, according to P.J. Creevy's
Adolphus Cooke (Longford, 1970), he had built,
at or near his house, Cookesborough,

a massive building sunk in the ground, with marble
steps leading down into it, and an arched roof lined
with marble slabs. It also had a beautiful arched fireplace at one end, a great brass lamp hanging from the
roof, and a huge marble chair with a back shaped like
an arch in front of which stood a reading desk with a
volume of the Holy Bible on it. There were shelves also
stocked with a large number of books. Mr Cooke
desired that when he died his body should be embalmed
and placed in a sitting position in the chair ...

The fire and the lamp were to receive 'daily
attention'.

The local clergyman, the Rev. Mr Lyster, did not approve of this arrangement, and Adolphus was put in the beehive vault which he had apparently built to receive the remains of his father and one of his half-brothers. He died in 1876, and the Cookesborough mausoleum was later demolished.

Not quite so odd as Mr Cooke, but odd enough, is Dr Edward Hudson, who left £500 by his will in 1822 for the erection in the churchyard at Ardnegihy (Glenville), Co. Cork, of 'a hollow cone or pyramid for performing his experiments on the pendulum and for elucidating the phenomena of comets, planets &c', desiring to be buried in the vault beneath it. History does not, so far, record whether this was done or not. At all events, no trace of it now remains.

It is, in the nature of things, unusual for a mausoleum to be demolished, unless it gets in the way of Sunday motoring in Co. Down. But as recently as 1962 the grand mausoleum of the Fitzmaurice family, Earls of Kerry, cylindrical, domed, and with outworks, which had the misfortune to stand on a cliff near Lixnaw where quarrying was in progress, was demolished. The owner sued the Kerry County Council for compensation and got it. But there is no compensation for us.

It is not unknown for a mausoleum to be left unfinished. The wonder is that it does not happen more often, when the chief instigator, who expects to lie in it, may die before it is ready and may leave, either not enough money, or an heir disinclined to spend it. Perhaps the most striking example is the Bruen mausoleum at Oakpark in Co. Carlow, designed by J.B. Keane as a peripteral Greek temple. Only the cella was in fact built. But even in its incomplete state it is one of the largest and most impressive in the country, and the ashlar masonry is of the highest quality, contrasting rather cruelly with the couple of insignificant-looking graves which seem to

be its only occupants. In another case, at
Killileagh near Doolin in Co. Clare, reported
by the late Billy English, the MacNamara
family built, in a field near the churchyard, a
mausoleum of channelled ashlar with a cor-
nice and architraved doorcase, but, for what-
ever reason, never moved in. It stands open,
with the door still swinging in the wind. The
same observer reported the mausoleum of the
Judge family near Mosstown, Co. Westmeath, who, though they lived in three houses
in King's County (Offaly), chose to build
their rather unimpressive shed-like structure,
formerly roofed with slate, in the middle of a
circular earthwork some miles to the north in
a different county.

There is no inscription at Mosstown,
but by way of compensation there is in the
Poems ... Serious and Diverting of Laurence
Whyte (Dublin, 1740), an 'Elegy on the most
lamented Death of Arthur Judge Senior', who
died in 1724 aged eighty-five. The verses

recite his virtues in the usual manner, and continue:

And though Britannia first to him gave breath
Britannia's sister must lament his death
Whom in his Youth she did adopt her child
And in her bosom long had reconcil'd,
Mosstown behold, his mansion house and seat
His first Plantation, and his last Retreat ...

After a recital of his virtues as a landlord, comes the Epitaph:

Here lies the Man whose Merit's so well known
It need not be recorded on a Stone.
Tradition shall a monument supply
For in Westmeath his name shall never die
But if a costly tomb we should bestow
And pay his Dust what we in Justice owe
Let this inscription from his Friend suffice
Which more than all our Elegy implies:
Beneath this marble honest Arthur Lies.

There are some marginal types of monument, not strictly mausolea, which should not be passed over. In the north-east, and to a lesser extent elsewhere, e.g., St Mullins in Co. Carlow, there are, in graveyards, rectangular enclosures with, in some cases, a frontispiece, and, in others, a wall at the back, architecturally treated, which are clearly related to the 'lairs' of Scotland, while in Kerry and parts of the adjoining counties there are cubical structures of more or less regular, sometimes unmortared, masonry which, with a little more elaboration and finish, and perhaps with a false door, could qualify to be called mausolea.

In the larger towns the big privately promoted cemeteries, following the example of Père Lachaise in Paris, were opened in Belfast (Clifton and Friar's Bush) and Dublin (Goldenbridge, Mount Jerome, Glasnevin) in the second quarter of the nineteenth century, and, like their Paris and London and Glasgow counterparts, they contain mausolea. There are parts of Mount Jerome in which one can easily imagine oneself to be in Père Lachaise, while the street of catacombs there has so many familiar names on the front doors of the vaults that one could almost be in some *outre-tombe* version of Grafton Street or Fitzwilliam Square.

The number of architects' names which can be attached to Irish mausolea is rather small: Pearce, Gandon, Adam and James Wyatt of course, with tentative attributions of one each to Thomas Cooley and John Aheron. At the latest count, Simon Vierpyl brings up the rear for the eighteenth century. In the nineteenth J.F. Fuller has the largest score with three and probably four, followed by George Ashlin with perhaps two, and J.B. Keane with one. James Brooks, William Fogerty, William Caldbeck and Slater & Carpenter are not names to conjure with.

Two of the very finest in architectural quality, Castlelyons and Ruan, have no known architect. Those by Pearce and by

Robert Adam are certainly in the first half-dozen. If Oughaval is indeed by Aheron it is much more exciting than anything else he did, and even if Vierpyl is responsible for only half of what we now see at Kilbride, Co. Wicklow, it is the major half. From then downwards it is up to the reader's personal taste, and will be much affected by the weather, the vegetation and his own mood when he finally gets to see the monument.

Whether the coffins in these mausolea are above ground or below, visible or invisible, it is safe to assume that in nearly every case there is a sealed lead coffin inside the wooden one. A nicely chiselled inscription on a small mausoleum in Co. Cavan says 'Lead coffins only Admitted'. But Nature, or in this case human nature, has a way of developing antibodies, and at the very moment when the mausoleum was at its apogee there were movements in a contrary sense. I have read somewhere of a bizarre garden-party, given

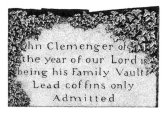

by, I think, the Duke of Sutherland in the grounds of Stafford House (now Lancaster House) in London some time in about the 1860s, to promote the use of wicker coffins. The fashionable ladies and gentlemen sauntered around the garden admiring the various models on display.

Such an initiative should surely be welcomed nowadays as ecologically sound. Wilfrid Scawen Blunt, we recall, though buried beneath an impeccably classical tomb, was lowered into the ground wrapped in an Arab blanket. Perhaps, as the icy grip of the morticians' cartel tightens on the emotionally vulnerable middle classes, and the squandering of energy in cremation becomes less and less acceptable, a movement in the opposite direction may gather momentum. 'Imperial Caesar, dead and gone to clay ...' Perhaps Lenin and Mao will be the last world figures 'to subsist in bones and be but pyramidally extant'?

Perhaps; but I doubt it.

ULSTER

This mausoleum, of the widely diffused half-up/half-down type, is in the graveyard of the Presbyterian church at Clough, between Newcastle and Downpatrick. Its form seems to owe something to that of the Graham mausoleum at Methven in Scotland, designed by James Playfair in 1793, the year before his untimely death. The Presbyterian association, as well as those of Playfair with the Townley Balfour family of Co. Louth, suggest some sort of influence. But the Clough mausoleum was not built until about 1860 and is much more elaborately decorated, in a rich blend of neoclassical and baroque.

Whether the alternation of pink and grey in the sandstone of which it is built is fully intentional or partly accidental is not easy to determine, as it is not completely consistent, though impossible not to notice.

I

MURLAND

Clough, Co. Down

Among the small lakes and little hills of the Cavan–Monaghan border close to Cootehill, not far from Bellamont Forest, in the thickly replanted demesne of the long-vanished Dartrey Castle, this mausoleum by James Wyatt is nowadays hard to find. Its chief glory is, or was, the sculptural group by Joseph Wilton to the memory of Lord Dartrey's first wife, who died in 1772.

When I first saw the mausoleum it still had a roof, but the door was blocked up. Since then the roof has collapsed and the monument has been damaged by vandals.

Potterton notes that notwithstanding Lord Dartrey's 'grateful sense of the blessings he enjoyed in such a wife', he had married an American lady, a granddaughter of William Penn, before Lady Anne had been dead a year or the monument even erected.

The artist has removed some trees to improve the view, and opened the door to give us a glimpse of what is within.

II

DAWSON

Dartrey, Co. Monaghan

In the Presbyterian graveyard on the side of a hill, this miniature Taj Mahal is built entirely of cut stone. One of the Stephenson family, who built it in 1837, was Superintending Surgeon of the Madras Presidency, and three other medical Stephensons are among the thirteen members of the family here interred. The mausoleum cost £300. Near it is a very orientalizing obelisk. Much overgrown until recent years, parts of it are still in a somewhat shaky condition, and not all of the pinnacles are in place. The graveyard is, very practically, kept cropped by sheep and commands a wide view to the south towards Belfast.

III

STEPHENSON
Kilbride, Co. Antrim

The Belfast–Bengal axis is one of the curiosities of the subject. This small group of mausolea at Knockbreda, which is now on the edge of Belfast, would not excite remark in South Park Street Cemetery in Calcutta. It is not immediately apparent what connexions the Greg, Rainey, Waddel Cunningham or Douglas families may have had with India, but, as with the Stephensons at Kilbride, some trading link may be suspected. The mausolea at Knockbreda have a strong family resemblance and, unlike that at Kilbride, are largely made of compo and have suffered in consequence. Within recent years one of those at Knockbreda has fallen victim to clerical enthusiasm for the accommodation of the motor-car.

The Cave Hill may be seen in the background, while overhead are evidences of the present discontents.

The church, of 1737, is by Richard Castle.

IV

GREG

Knockbreda, Co. Down

Unlike any other Irish mausoleum, and later than most, it is approached by a very long avenue of yews but is hard to find in its dramatic setting on the edge of a cliff in the Rossmore demesne. With a high sprocketed roof of red tiles, which make an awkward junction with the cylindrical tower at the east end, it has a pointed west door above which there is a bracketed shelf, perhaps for a bell. The east window, with its steep gable, projects, also awkwardly, from the tower, which is crowned with a stone dome.

The vast house of the Westenra family, Lords Rossmore, was frequently added to in the nineteenth century but demolished some twenty years ago after falling into picturesque ruin. The mausoleum, of the late nineteenth or early twentieth century, has been tentatively attributed to Fuller.

V

WESTENRA

Rossmore, Co. Monaghan

In the graveyard adjoining Castle Upton at Templepatrick, Co. Antrim, this is virtually the only building in all Ireland by any of the family of Adam. The elegant mausoleum and the Castle Upton stables constitute almost all Robert Adam's Irish *œuvre*. Clotworthy Upton succeeded his brother in 1768, and soon after coming to live at Castle Upton, probably after 1772, commissioned Adam to do proposals for the house and also to design the mausoleum in memory of his elder brother and predecessor. It seems not to have been built until 1789. The motif of the main elevation is the familiar neoclassical 'triumphal arch' theme, frequently employed by James Gandon also. On the walls separating the gardens from the mausoleum peacocks strike decorative attitudes, emitting unmelodious shrieks.

VI

UPTON

Templepatrick, Co. Antrim

MUNSTER

Charles Bianconi, the penniless pedlar who built up a great transport empire in the 1840s, and lived at Longfield House just across the river Suir, built this funerary chapel for himself twenty years before he died. 'Unaided by an architect,' says his great-niece and biographer, 'he and his head carpenter, Bob Noble, had managed to erect a solid, if unorthodox, little building in limestone and grey sandstone, with the help of some local artisans.' It occupies a large plot beside the Catholic church. 'The body of his wife Kate was brought back from Italy to rest beneath a bas-relief by Benzoni of her reclining effigy in Italian marble.' It was consecrated by the Archbishop of Cashel in 1857, and Bianconi himself died and was buried in it in 1875.

VII

BIANCONI

Boherlahan, Co. Tipperary

James Barry, the fourth Earl of Barrymore, died in 1747 at the age of eighty, and his son the fifth Earl, also James, followed him only four years later. This mausoleum, which is primarily a setting for the lofty pedimented monument by David Sheehan and John Houghton, seems to date from about 1753. The pedimented centrepiece, in brick with stone dressings, is flanked by rubble-stone walls, and the whole is finished by hipped roofs in slate. There are oculi framed in brick in the side walls. All the openings have wrought-iron grilles, and the opening grille or gate in the centre is particularly fine. A separate stairs at the side leads down to the vault. This mausoleum has been well cared for.

There is another mausoleum in the graveyard, clearly inspired by the Barry one, but simpler and with pointed-arch openings. The whole is dominated by the vast ivy-clad ruin of the 'castle'.

VIII

BARRY

Castlelyons, Co. Cork

Rivalling that of Sir Michael O'Loghlen at Ruan in solidity (*see plate XI*), the Bindon Scott mausoleum at Killadysert on the estuary of the river Fergus has a sturdy Doric portico *in antis*, and is magnificently set off by the slender mediæval west tower of the ruined church in whose graveyard it stands. The graveyard, like some others in this part of the country, is well tended. The Bindons were a large clan in this part of Clare, as Bindon Scott, Bindon Blood and just plain Bindon. This particular lot lived at Cahircon, three miles to the south.

The mausoleum was erected in 1837 by John Bindon Scott of Cahircon and John Scott of Creevagh to the memory of their fathers and also for themselves and their posterity. Round the sides and back it is more cheaply finished, unlike that of Sir Michael O'Loghlen. It has a cast-iron two-leaf door. There are two more house-shaped tombs in the graveyard.

IX

BINDON SCOTT

Killadysert, Co. Clare

William Smith O'Brien, son of Sir Lucius O'Brien of Dromoland, Co. Clare, led the abortive insurrection of 1848 which ended in the defeat at the 'Cabbage Patch' and a death sentence, commuted to transportation. Allowed to return from Tasmania in 1854 at the age of fifty-one, he died in Wales ten years later. His mausoleum, inscribed 'Pro Libertate Patriae', signed at one end by William Fogerty, architect, of Dublin, and at the other by James Cavanagh, builder, of Limerick, contains also his wife Lucy Caroline, who predeceased him by three years, and his eldest son Edward William, 'a just man, a lover of his people, 1837–1909'. I find this use of the possessive 'his' interesting in the context. In the romanesque style later used in the nearby O'Brien family house, Cahirmoyle, by J.J. McCarthy, the Rathronan mausoleum is enriched by the use of coloured marbles. The Vandeleur mausoleum at Kilrush, Co. Clare, ten years later, is similar.

X

SMITH O'BRIEN

Rathronan, Co. Limerick

Probably the finest example of the Egyptian style in the funerary line in all Ireland, the mausoleum of Sir Michael O'Loghlen bursts upon the astonished spectator in the otherwise unremarkable graveyard of the Catholic church in Ruan, an obscure place in the middle of Co. Clare, some five miles north of Ennis. It is clearly the tomb of a local boy who made good. And indeed Sir Michael, who was born in 1789, was a man of outstanding ability: O'Connell's legal understudy, a great success at the bar, and ultimately Master of the Rolls, the first Catholic judge and the first Catholic law officer in modern times. He died in 1842, and was one of the very few whose statue adorned the great central hall of the Four Courts before the destruction of 1922. But his mausoleum has survived.

XI

O'LOGHLEN

Ruan, Co. Clare

LEINSTER

Conspicuous from the road, in the grounds of the Catholic church, this mausoleum or memorial chapel looks much later than its date, which is 1818. The family's arms are in the panel over the door, and past glories are rehearsed in the rectangular panels on the sides.

The church adjoining, by Pugin and Ashlin, is nearly fifty years later (1865), but much of a date with the mausoleum is Gracefield, four miles to the north-west, a picturesque house in the villa style by William Robertson of Kilkenny, who adapted a design by John Nash, retrenching it in the process.

XII

G R A C E

Arless, Co. Laois

The village of Carbury has a variety of attractions: the mediæval castle of the Berminghams on its hill; Newberry Hall, a handsome mid-eighteenth-century house; a Protestant church surrounded with old trees, and, between it and the castle, this mausoleum of the Colleys or Cowleys. It was they who converted the castle and later passed the property to the Pomeroy family, who built Newberry Hall and also, we must suppose, the mausoleum. They were later ennobled as Lord Harberton, while the Colleys changed their name to Wesley or Wellesley and produced the Duke of Wellington.

The mausoleum has a barrel-vaulted roof. All the interments are underneath the floor, and the doorway lies open, facing the castle. On the left are the ruins of the mediæval church. Of the six obelisk finials on the mausoleum only three now stand, and the ivy is busy with the rest.

XIII

POMEROY

Carbury, Co. Kildare

This most elegant three-sided pyramid seems to have been put up in about 1814, when Godwin Swifte of Lionsden, who had in about 1803 married his cousin Sophia Jane Swift, thus adding an 'e' to her name, died. She married, in 1816, Comte Lepelettier de Molandé, who in turn died some time before 1829. During all this time she was the adored of Walter Savage Landor, who addressed to her, under the name 'Ianthe' (derived from Jane), the best of his love poetry. When she died at Versailles in 1851, thirteen years before Landor, her body was brought back to Castlerickard. There are two coffins in the vault, the larger presumably Godwin's and the smaller Ianthe's. The vault has now been sealed, one hopes for ever, and the pyramid put in good order.

XIV

SWIFTE

Castlerickard, Co. Meath

Considering that its architect was one of the greatest who ever worked in Ireland, this building is something of a disappointment. For one thing, it is dwarfishly low, seeming hardly to emerge from the earth, and there is little reason to suppose that it was ever otherwise. The elements of which it is composed, though adroitly put together, are the typical Gandonian clichés: paterae, husk-ropes and the like, so familiar from his greater buildings. And the way in which it is tacked on to the south wall of the east end of the church is not happy, even when allowance is made for the nineteenth-century addition of the chancel.

The interior of the church, except for the east end and the ceiling, is much as Gandon left it, and of greater interest.

XV

PORTARLINGTON

Coolbanagher, Co. Laois

In the Church of Ireland graveyard at Drumcar, the mausoleum of the McClintock family, whose eighteenth-century house is close by, was designed by Slater and Carpenter, who also added the chancel of the church. The little niches accommodate shields of arms and only the central one is pierced to ventilate the interior. The hexagonal pyramid roof is slated but at present in good repair, though the family no longer occupy the house. Major H.F. McClintock the antiquary lived here.

The hexagon or octagon was popular in mid-Victorian times: another, larger, example is at Headfort, Co. Meath, by John Franklin Fuller, of 1869.

XVI

McCLINTOCK

Drumcar, Co. Louth

Sited on a slope overlooking the Benedictine abbey and other ecclesiastical ruins which together make up the 'town' of Fore (renowned for its 'seven wonders'), a mediæval anchorite's cell like a tiny tower-house, complete with fireplace and loo, was adapted by George Ashlin in 1867 to form the chancel of a mortuary chapel for the Greville family, who had married the last of the Nugents who were Earls of Westmeath.

Among several memorial slabs preserved here is that of the last hermit, Patrick Beglan or Begley (ob. 1616), and another recording the building or adaptation of the cell by Richard, Earl of Westmeath, in 1680, nearly two hundred years before the remodelling for the Grevilles.

XVII

GREVILLE NUGENT

Fore, Co. Westmeath

The base of the mediæval tower, in the form of a square turning into an octagon, and closely resembling that at Askeaton, Co. Limerick, serves as a mausoleum to contain the bodies of several members of the Tighe family of Woodstock, the ruined house on the hill above the town, who also owned Rosanna, Co. Wicklow. Mary Tighe, the author of the once famous but now almost forgotten poem *Psyche*, unhappily married to her cousin William Tighe, died of consumption aged twenty-eight in 1810 and has a mausoleum all to herself, the severe neo-classical cube to the left of the tower. It contains 'a full-length recumbent effigy of the poetess, her head resting on a cushion, and a winged Genius of Poetry seated at her ear' (Potterton) by Flaxman. Perched on her shoulder like a pet cat, it is an addition probably by another hand.

XVIII

TIGHE

Inistioge, Co. Kilkenny

Richard Malone, the elder brother of the famous Shakespearean critic Edmund Malone, was born between 1736 and 1741, was created Lord Sunderlin in 1785, and died in 1816. He built the church with its charming carpenter's gothick interior, now mostly fallen into ruin, and is buried under this pyramid, one of many that took a hint from the reconstructions of Queen Artemisia's original mausoleum at Halicarnassus (though on a vastly smaller scale), being a pyramid on a podium rather than one rising straight from the ground. The Stratford mausoleum at Baltinglass is another instance, but there the podium is much more massive than the pyramid which sits on top. The interior has a cross vault supporting the superincumbent masonry, with three black sarcophagi in niches, and another vault beneath.

No designer is known for either Kilbixy church or the Malone tomb.

XIX

MALONE

Kilbixy, Co. Westmeath

In an old graveyard on the south-east edge of the Shelton Abbey estate (Shelton Abbey is now a gaol), this is one of the most romantic and mysterious of Irish mausolea. Not that there is any mystery about its construction. As the inscription on the sarcophagus records, it was erected in 1785 by Ralph Howard, Viscount Wicklow, as a place of burial for his family and in memory of Mrs Dorothea Howard, who died in 1684 (*sic*) and is buried nearby: and it is known to have been designed by Simon Vierpyl, whom Lord Charlemont brought from Italy to Dublin. And very elegant it is. No: the mystery is that below and in front of it is that curious façade in granite with more than a whiff of the Egyptian taste about it, which must surely be later and is even perhaps of a different family. Though it looks as if it may have carried an inscription, such is the condition of the granite that the lettering defies decipherment.

XX

HOWARD

Kilbride, Co. Wicklow

Humewood, near the village of Kiltegan, is one of the two or three most extreme of Irish Victorian houses. It was designed by William White for William Wentworth Fitzwilliam Hume Dick and begun in 1867. (Appearances to the contrary notwithstanding, it seems that he was unconnected with his neighbour Charles William Wentworth, Earl Fitzwilliam: the family kept changing their name from Hume to Dick and back again, at one point calling themselves Hume Hume.)

The house was completed by 1870, but the ensuing lawsuit between the architect and the builder, both English, did not end till 1876. The builder won. By then another architect, James Brooks, also English, had made substantial additions to the already large house, and he also, as Jeanne Sheehy has established, designed this massive mausoleum, which stands in the Church of Ireland churchyard.

XXI

HUME DICK

Kiltegan, Co. Wicklow

One of the most extraordinary mausolea of all. In a (now) well-kept graveyard a few miles from Stradbally, it was until recently almost invisible, so densely shrouded in ivy that, apart from guessing that it was an eighteenth-century structure standing on top of the vaulted eastern limb of a ruined mediæval church, it was difficult to make sense of it. Except, of course, for the evident fact that most of the undercroft was occupied by an enormous stone sarcophagus with the arms of Cosby containing—what? one coffin? or several? or none at all? Who knows? The coat of arms has now been picked out in bright colours including some aluminium paint.

The stone barrel-vault of the mausoleum is also the external roof, and the battlements vaguely resemble the Irish stepped variety. It was apparently designed by John Aheron, the author of the first book on architecture to be published in Ireland.

XXII

C O S B Y

Oughaval, Co. Laois

This country graveyard a few miles north of Dublin was favoured by the Morgan family, rich Catholic merchants of the city. There are two mausolea, both now roofless. The more serious of the two, on the right of the picture, has an armorial tablet over the door reading 'Andreas Morgan Mercator Dublinensis hoc monumentum pro sua familia fieri testamentum mandavit Filii ejus optimo merentes posuerunt Andreas obiit 3 Martii 1746'. Another tablet commemorates Colum B Morgan of Usher's Island in the City of Dublin, 1790.

It had a frieze of metopes and triglyphs, now much decayed; but two well-carved metopes of a winged figure and an hourglass are still *in situ*.

One of the gothic arches has a label-stop which looks suspiciously like a re-used mediæval carving of a head. The activity discernible in the background indicates the proximity of Dublin Airport.

XXIII

MORGAN

St Margaret's, Co. Dublin

There is a design by Sir Edward Lovett Pearce for this obelisk-mausoleum in the Stillorgan album at Elton Hall, in two drawings, one endorsed 'Lady Allen's burying-place, to be a monument of patience'. Pearce had a house on the Allen estate and lived on close terms with the family. Whether Lady Allen, born Margaret Du Pass, or any other of the Allens was in the end buried here or not, the mausoleum was built, and in a somewhat grander style than that of the original design. It is raised on a massive base of rockwork, elaborately planned with a central domical compartment and four external staircases, in the manner of Bernini. Like some other Irish mausolea, it stood by itself in the demesne.

The house at Stillorgan is long gone, and aside from part of a sunken garden and a long domed grotto, also by Pearce, nothing remains of the Allens' improvements except the obelisk.

XXIV

ALLEN

Stillorgan, Co. Dublin

CONNACHT

Close to Laurencetown with its Volunteer gateway and gothick eyecatchers, this mausoleum of the Seymour family stands just outside the old graveyard, in front of and well in sight of the house, which is an eighteenth-century house attached to a mediæval tower-house. This one is unusual in having an 'apron' in front of the main structure and a flight of steps leading down to the usual iron door. The upper part is openwork and apparently never contained anything. Something similar is to be seen at the Kelly tomb by the roadside near Ruan, Co. Clare, where a sunken way leads to a door in the base of a little artificial hill with an open feature standing on top. Openwork structures are found at Belleek, Co. Mayo (gothic), Emper, Co. Westmeath, and Movilla, Co. Down (classic), but do not qualify as mausolea.

XXV

SEYMOUR

Ballymore, Co. Galway

In some ways the most remarkable of all, this tiny mortuary chapel is squeezed in between two shops in the main street of the town. Entirely constructed of selected and contrasting stone and regardless of expense, it was built by Mr Edward Costello for the reception of his wife, who died in 1877, and subsequently of himself.

Beneath the floor and visible through thick plate glass the two coffins lie side by side. The mausoleum is well cared for and the door is normally kept open so that it is seen by many of those who pass through the town while cruising on river or canal.

On grounds of style and date, Jeremy Williams suggests that the designer may have been George Ashlin, the partner and successor of A.W.N. Pugin.

XXVI

COSTELLO

Carrick-on-Shannon, Co. Leitrim

Considering that there are cast-iron churches in the tropics, and cast-iron bridges exported in parts from England and Scotland, to be assembled on site, not to mention home-grown cast-iron tombstones in Co. Laois, and perhaps elsewhere, it is surprising that there are not more cast-iron mausolea.

This one, of Colonel Maurice Dennis of Bermingham House, was probably cast in Scotland by the Carron Ironworks or some such firm. The inscriptions were not cast integrally with the building, but in strip form riveted in place. The mausoleum is evidently modelled on the choragic monument of Lysicrates in Athens, a very popular prototype, much used for the tops of church towers as well as for tombs.

Colonel Dennis died in 1863, and over a hundred years later the door of the mausoleum was ajar and one could see his coffin sitting on the floor.

XXVII

DENNIS

Clonbern, Co. Galway

On the bleak shore of Galway Bay, within sight of the ruined Tyrone House of the St George family, this gaunt mausoleum is attached as a quasi-transept to the mediæval, and as usual ruined, church of Drumacoo. It is resonant with literary references. The house, and the St Georges, are credibly reported to have been the models for Somerville and Ross's novel *The Big House at Inver*, while the mausoleum itself is, with less certainty, pointed to as the original of that in which, in John Betjeman's poem, the 'fantastic mausoleum'

> Sings its own seablown Te Deum
> In and out the slipping slates.

There is nothing particularly fantastic about the mausoleum except that the window-tracery is of cast iron. The St Georges are all under the pavement and the slates are no longer slipping.

XXVIII

ST GEORGE

Drumacoo, Co. Galway

The town of Carrick-on-Shannon can boast two sharply contrasting mausolea: that of the Costellos in its unusual urban situation (*see plate XXVI*) and this one, of the ubiquitous St George family, just on the edge of town, in a railed enclosure, itself in the garden of Hatley Manor. The vermiculated stonework and the openwork cast-iron piers of the enclosure catch the eye, but are outshone by the grandiloquent armorial display in the stone stele which surmounts the doric porch, boasting no fewer than sixteen heraldic quarterings.

Jeremy Williams suggests that the designer was William Caldbeck.

XXIX

ST GEORGE

Hatley Manor, Co. Leitrim

Though not in the strictest sense a mausoleum, because it has nothing in the semblance of a door, the Bingham tomb at Hollymount, five miles east-north-east of Ballinrobe, is so large and such a fine piece of architecture and so finely wrought that we could not forbear to include it.

The setting is one of pleasing decay. The now roofless church with its openwork spire is decaying gracefully, and so is Hollymount House a few hundred yards away. The church is of 1816, the house somewhat earlier. The Binghams lived not here but at Newbrook, five or six miles to the north, which was burnt in 1837 and never rebuilt. The inscriptions are long and interesting: see the Introduction.

XXX

BINGHAM

Hollymount, Co. Mayo

A miniature tower-house now hidden in conifer plantations—ironically since it stood originally in what was said to be an 'indigenous' oak forest—contains the tombs of Robert ffrench and his daughter Kathleen in a semi-subterranean vault, and a memorial chapel over it, vaulted in granite. It was built with his wife's Russian money, but he died in Italy and was brought back to Monivea. The architect was supposedly Francis Persse, Lady Gregory's brother—or perhaps, as Jeremy Williams suggests, really George Ashlin?—and the date 1897–1901. It is now very well kept by the local people, and in ecclesiastical use.

XXXI

FFRENCH

Monivea, Co. Galway

The two mausolea at Tulsk are picturesquely tucked in among the fragments of the Dominican friary. They are rather obviously in competition with one another: the larger and more northerly one, of the Grace family, dated 1868, and the other, of Taaffe, 1872. Grace seems to have won the contest, being fully above ground, while Taaffe is half-sunken. When first visited, some twenty years ago, one could walk into both of them, among the coffins which were lying about, in perfect decency, on the floor. But in a recent visit the Grace mausoleum was empty, and the iron door of Taaffe's either jammed or locked: just as well, perhaps, in view of the decline of piety in recent years.

Just across the road is a particularly splendid example of a rural ball-alley, complete with grandstand and vomitoria, all in poured concrete.

XXXII

GRACE *and* TAAFFE

Tulsk, Co. Roscommon

Visible from the MGWR line to Galway, half a mile to the north-east of Woodlawn station, this is the largest mausoleum in Ireland, at least in area. A circular wall with crenellations and loops encloses a sizeable plot in the middle of which stands the circular tower, with an entrance at ground-floor level but no floor or stairs. In the middle of the 'keep' is the tomb of Frederick Trench of Woodlawn, who died in 1797 and is credited with being the builder of the mausoleum.

Among the numerous Trench graves in the enclosure is that of Dudley Oliver Trench, fifth Lord Ashtown, who died in 1979. The original had twelve—or twenty-one?—children, which is sometimes given as the reason for his having built such a large mausoleum; but this was such a common circumstance that it hardly seems adequate.

XXXIII

TRENCH

Woodlawn, Co. Galway

INDEX

Place names corresponding to plates are given in small capitals, with Ordnance Survey reference numbers in brackets.

INDEX

INDEX

INDEX

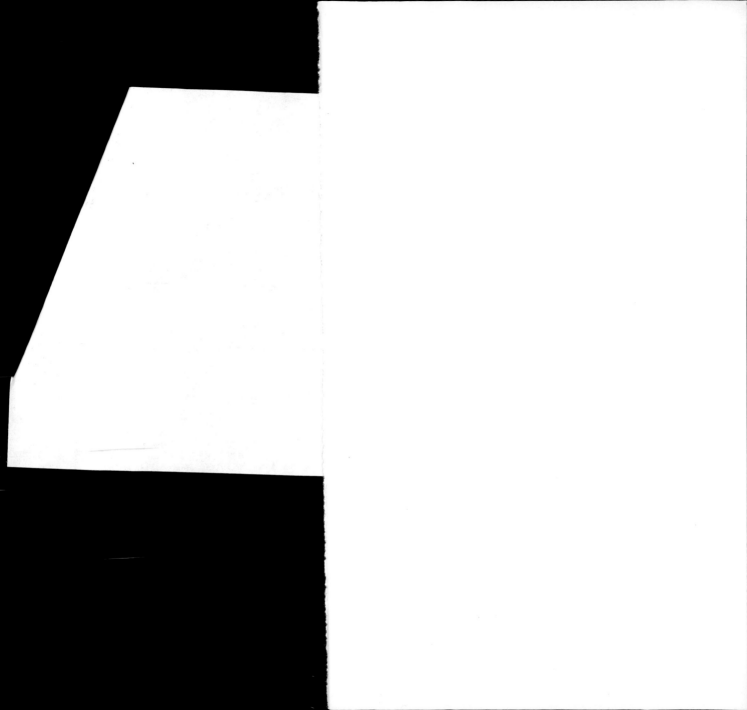